Spiralizer
Recipe Book

Spiralizer Recipes for

WEIGHT LOSS, ANTI-AGING, ANTI-INFLAMMATORY

& So Much More!

STEPHANIE SHAW

Disclaimer

Summary

There are ways to make your meals exciting and visually delectable without heading out to fine dining restaurants. The key is hidden in the way you prepare the fruits and vegetables for your meals.

The Spiralizer offers you the opportunity to prepare your fruits and vegetables differently, transforming each meal into a unique experience. The visual appearance of your food goes a long way to attract the attention of people. The Spiralizer makes it possible for you to introduce novelty to traditional recipes, making them instant hits with your family and guests.

This eBook aims to illuminate you about the possibilities of using the Spiralizer for greater benefits. The next few pages will inform you about the advantages of using the Spiralizer to prepare your fruits and vegetables, helping you transform your meals into exciting feasts!

So keep reading to find out everything you need to know about the Spiralizer and how it can help you in your daily routine!

Table of Contents

Chapter 1 – Introduction to Spiralizer

There aren't many options available to you when it comes to cutting the fruits and vegetables for your meals. It's usually the dices, cuboids, julienne, or some of the random shapes, which are natural for different fruits and vegetables. It doesn't have to be this way anymore! The Spiralizer is here to offer a special 'twist' to your meals!

I discovered the Spiralizer quite recently while shopping for the latest kitchen utensils. This piece of kitchen equipment is apparently quite popular with mothers. It is like the typical grater we have at our homes except that the cutters/blades in this case are different. When you turn the lever, you are able to cut the fruit/vegetable in spirals of varying thickness and size (depending on the cutter/blade you use). What you get in the end is an exciting, non-conventional cut for your natural ingredients!

I was particularly surprised about how easy it is to use and how it transforms the regular meals into visually exciting feasts. It does not require any effort to set up the system. All you need to do is decide which vegetables or fruits to spiralize, place them in the holder and twist the lever. What you get at the other side can really provide a necessary twist to your meals – quite literally as well!

On top of this, it is absolutely simple to clean and maintain. Remember to detach the blades so you don't end up injuring your hand. Wash it thoroughly with water and dish washing soap. Use a brush if you feel necessary. Let it dry on the dish stand and it will be ready to store in your cupboard, strategically away from plain sight!

It has helped me include a higher quantity of nutritious fruits and vegetables in my everyday meals. Not only this, it has transformed each mealtime into a much anticipated moment of the day as I observe my family enjoying their meals even more!

Chapter 2 – Benefits of Spiralized Fruits and Vegetables

Spiralized fruits and vegetables do not just make your meals look attractive. There are several other benefits to incorporating them in your daily meals.

Do you need grain free pasta? The Spiralizer will help you convert any and every vegetable into spaghetti-like strands that can be used in place of regular flour-based pasta. You don't even need to boil it – provided you are not using any vegetables that are meant to be cooked before consumption. You can enjoy flavor-rich, gluten-free alternatives to grain pasta, which would be excellent for those on a Paleo, vegan or vegetarian diet.

Spiralized vegetables do not only help you tackle gluten sensitivities, they also help you cut down on your carbohydrate intake which definitely contributes to weight loss, because the calories you are consuming are much lower in the case of vegetables as compared to the pasta made from grain. You will also be able to maintain the weight you have shed as long as you continue to have spiralized vegetables in place of grain pasta.

When you replace your carbohydrate-laden meals with spiralized vegetables, your meals will be more nutritious and therefore healthier for you. If you have diabetes, this will help considerably in ensuring you maintain normal blood glucose levels.

Having meals that are prepared with spiralized vegetables will help you to detoxify your body because of the high water content in vegetables. This is one of the reasons why those who switch to eating more vegetables, especially raw vegetables or very lightly cooked vegetables, find themselves feeling more energetic, they have clearer skin, and generally feel healthier.

If you have children, they will absolutely love to spiralize the vegetables and fruits; this encourages them to eat what they have prepared. The spiralizer is safe for them to use as long as they are being closely supervised. It is a very good way of introducing them to new vegetables. They will enjoy the variety and if they get to pick the blades, it adds to their creativity

It is beneficial for the seniors as well. Serving small portions of attractive looking meals will encourage them to eat. The different blades make it possible to slice fruits and vegetables at varying thickness, which will ease the preparation and production of a visually attractive meal. The smaller blades will produce easier to chew vegetables and fruit and will be especially beneficial to those with dental problems.

With the spiralizer, you will find that your creative impulses will be stimulated. Different blades and cutters also mean a greater variety of cuts that go with different recipes and preparations. So when I prepare spaghetti for kids, I use the tighter and smaller spirals to go with the texture of the recipe. And when I am preparing salads, I use fuller spirals to create flowers and rings. You can customize the shape and size according to the overall look and feel of your recipe!

That gives you plenty of reason to try out the spiralizer and turn your meal times into exciting feasts. It is fun, easy, and healthy! So what are you still waiting for?

Chapter 3 – Best Fruits and Vegetables to Spiralize

As a general rule of thumb, firm vegetables and fruits are the best ones to spiralize. This includes root vegetables like carrots, sweet potatoes, courgette and others. Besides this, you'll find spiralizing apples, cucumbers, squash and pumpkin to be quite exciting as well.

It has a lot to do with the texture and firmness of the fruits and vegetables you choose. Also, the size of the ingredient will make it easier (or more difficult) to manage. Keeping these key considerations in mind, you can pick up just about any fruit and vegetable from the farmer's store that is fresh, seasonally relevant and spiralizer-friendly.

Here's a starter's list to give you an idea about how it works. These are some of the fruits and vegetables you can spiralize with ease.

- Carrots
- Sweet Potatoes
- Courgette
- Apples
- Cucumbers
- Squash
- Pumpkin
- Zucchini
- White Potato
- Beet
- Rutabaga
- Parsnip
- Jicama
- Radish
- Onion

Still confused about what to spiralize? Here's the check list I use to decide whether I should be spiralizing the fruits and vegetables or not.

- ✓ Vegetables and fruits with a tough core, seeds, or a hollow center pose difficulty in spiralizing.
- ✓ They need to be at least 1.5" in diameter in order to be spiralized with ease.
- ✓ Fruits and Vegetables shorter than 2" in length are extremely difficult to spiralize.
- ✓ The ingredients need to be firm. Juicy and squishy fruits and vegetables cannot be spiralized.

So if you pick a fruit and/or vegetable and it does not meet the requirements mentioned above, it'll be better to pick another natural ingredient instead. For best results, use the spiralizer to cut fruits and vegetables that complement the tool!

Chapter 4 – 10 Spiralized Fruit and Vegetable Recipes for Children

Kids love spiralizing fruits and vegetables, just like they adore consuming such delicacies. Here are a few easy-to-make spiralized fruit and vegetable recipes for children.

Spiralized Zucchini Pasta with Italian Seasoning

Servings: 3-4

Ingredients

- 2 zucchinis tightly spiralized to resemble spaghetti
- 1 tomato roughly chopped
- 1 bell pepper roughly chopped
- 5 baby carrots roughly chopped
- 2 tbsp fresh thyme
- 1 tsp fresh oregano
- Salt and black pepper to taste

Instructions

1. Mix all the ingredients (other than spiralized zucchini) in a blender.
2. Blend the mixture to your desired consistency.
3. Adjust seasoning according to taste.
4. Pour it over the spiralized zucchini and serve.

Nutritional Information

- Calories - 48
- Carbohydrates - 10g - (3%)
- Protein - 3g - (6%)
- Total Fat - 1g - (2%)
- Sodium - 81mg - (3%)
- Fiber - 3g - (12%)

Percent Daily Values are based on a 2000 calorie diet.

Spiralized Zucchini with Peanut Sauce

Servings: 3-4

Ingredients

- 2 zucchini spiralized with the fine blade.
- 1 1/2 cup (200g) medium thickness spiralized jicama

For Peanut Sauce:

- 1/2 cup (130g) peanut butter
- 1/3 cup (80ml) orange juice
- 4-6 tbsp maple syrup
- 2-3 tbsp sesame oil
- 1/4 tsp ginger finely ground

Instructions

For Peanut Sauce:

1. Mix all the ingredients and blend well.
2. Store in an airtight container for later.

For the Recipe:

1. Place the spiralized zucchini and jicama in a serving plate.
2. Drench the vegetables in the peanut sauce.
3. Serve immediately.

Nutritional Information

- Calories - 458
- Carbohydrates - 39g - (13%)
- Protein - 13g - (26%)
- Total Fat - 31g - (48%)
- Sodium - 213mg - (9%)
- Fiber - 7g - (28%)

Percent Daily Values are based on a 2000 calorie diet.

Cucumber Wraps

Servings: 3-4

Ingredients

- 2 cucumbers spiralized using the broad blades.
- 1 carrot tightly spiralized
- 1 bell pepper julienned

For seasoning:

- 2-3 tbsp mustard paste
- 2-3 tbsp agave syrup
- 2-3 tbsp orange juice

Instructions

For the seasoning:

1. Mix all ingredients. Whisk thoroughly and set aside.

For Cucumber Wraps:

1. Spiralize the cucumbers length-wise at paper-thin thickness.
2. Wrap the bell pepper and carrots in the middle of cucumber wraps.
3. Drizzle the seasoning over the wraps and enjoy!

Nutritional Information

- Calories - 96
- Carbohydrates - 18g - (6%)
- Protein - 2g - (4%)
- Total Fat - 2g - (3%)
- Sodium - 66mg - (3%)
- Fiber - 4g - (16%)

Percent Daily Values are based on a 2000 calorie diet.

Multi-Colored Noodles Salad

Servings: 3-4

Ingredients

- 2 orange carrots tightly spiralized
- 2 maroon carrots tightly spiralized
- 1 apple tightly spiralized
- 1 parsnip tightly spiralized
- 2 spring onions julienned
- 1/3 cup (50g) toasted cashew nuts roughly chopped

For the dressing:

- 1 tbsp apple cider vinegar
- 1 tbsp maple syrup
- 2-3 tbsp olive oil
- Salt and pepper to taste

Instructions

1. Mix vinegar, maple syrup, olive oil, salt and pepper in a bowl and leave aside for use later.
2. Place all the remaining ingredients, apart from the pecans, into a bowl.
3. Pour the dressing over the vegetables. Marinate for about 30 minutes in the refrigerator.
4. Dish into a serving bowl, sprinkle the cashew nuts over the salad and serve.

Nutritional Information

- Calories - 269
- Carbohydrates - 29g - (10%)
- Protein - 4g - (8%)
- Total Fat - 17g - (26%)
- Sodium - 217mg - (9%)
- Fiber - 5g - (20%)

Percent Daily Values are based on a 2000 calorie diet.

Basic Spiralized Vegetable Soup

Servings: 4-6

Ingredients

- 4 cups (1 litre) of chicken/vegetable broth
- 1 carrot medium spiralized
- 1 celery stick sliced
- 1 bell pepper sliced
- 1 zucchini medium spiralized
- 1/4 cup (50g) chickpeas
- 2 garlic cloves finely chopped
- 1 medium sized onion finely chopped
- 1 tsp fresh basil leaves chopped
- 1 tsp olive oil
- Salt and black pepper to taste

Instructions

1. Heat the olive oil gently in a pan.
2. Saute the garlic and onion till fragrant.
3. Add the broth to the pan and bring to the boil.
4. Add all the vegetables to the saucepan.
5. Cook for about 10-15 minutes; or until the vegetables are tender.
6. Dish into a serving bowl, season with the salt and pepper.
7. Garnish with the chopped basil and serve.

Nutritional Information

- Calories - 146
- Carbohydrates - 19g - (6%)
- Protein - 8g - (16%)
- Total Fat - 4g - (6%)
- Cholesterol - 7mg - (2%)
- Sodium - 433mg - (18%)
- Fiber - 3g - (12%)

Percent Daily Values are based on a 2000 calorie diet.

Tangy Mixed Vegetable Salad

Servings: 3-4

Ingredients

- 1 zucchini tightly spiralized
- 1 carrot tightly spiralized
- 1 bell pepper sliced
- 1/4 cup (25g) peas boiled
- 1/4 cup (40g) corn boiled
- 1/2 cup (100g) mayonnaise
- 2-3 tbsp lemon juice
- Salt and black pepper to taste

Instructions

1. Mix all the ingredients thoroughly in a bowl.
2. Dish into a serving bowl and serve cold.

Nutritional Information

- Calories - 299
- Carbohydrates - 13g - (4%)
- Protein - 3g - (6%)
- Total Fat - 27g - (42%)
- Cholesterol - 13mg - (4%)
- Sodium - 349mg - (15%)
- Fiber - 3g - (12%)

Percent Daily Values are based on a 2000 calorie diet.

Raw Zucchini Twist with Shrimps

Servings: 3-4

Ingredients

- 2-3 medium sized zucchini tightly spiralized
- salt
- 18oz (500g) shrimp lightly cooked
- 1 medium sized carrots tightly spiralized
- 1/2 cabbage shredded
- 1-2 tbsp fresh mint finely chopped
- 2 tbsp fresh cilantro roughly chopped
- 2-3 tbsp roasted peanuts crushed
- 3/4 cup (180ml) coconut milk
- 1 small avocado chopped

For Sauce:

- 3-4 tbsp peanut butter
- 2 tsp low-sodium soy sauce
- 1/2 tbsp brown sugar
- 1 tsp vinegar
- Water as required

Instructions

For the Sauce:

1. Mix all the sauce ingredients thoroughly in a bowl. Set aside.

For the Twist:

1. Sprinkle salt on the spiralized zucchini and let it stand for 30 minutes in order to extract the fluid from the zucchini and drain the liquid.
2. Place the zucchini and the other vegetables into a serving bowl and add the coconut milk to the bowl.
3. Place the cooked shrimps on the vegetables.

4. Top off with the sauce, garnish with the chopped peanuts and herbs and serve.

Nutritional Information

- Calories - 587
- Carbohydrates - 28g - (9%)
- Protein - 56g - (112%)
- Total Fat - 31g - (48%)
- Cholesterol - 343mg - (114%)
- Sodium - 1376mg - (57%)
- Fiber - 9g - (36%)

Percent Daily Values are based on a 2000 calorie diet.

Spiralized Zucchini Soup with Mushrooms

Servings: 3-4

Ingredients

- 4 cups (1 litre) chicken/vegetable broth
- 2 zucchinis tightly spiralized
- 2 cups (135g) of green leafy vegetables (you can use kale leaves, spinach, spring greens or chard)
- 4 cups (280g) mushrooms chopped
- 1 tbsp garlic finely chopped
- 1 tbsp sesame oil
- 1 tbsp olive oil
- Salt and black pepper to taste

Instructions

1. Heat the olive gently in a pan.
2. Saute the garlic and ginger till fragrant.
3. Add the broth to the pan and bring to the boil.
4. Add the remaining ingredients (except the spiralized zucchini) to the broth.

5. Simmer for 4-6 minutes.
6. Add the zucchini and sesame oil before turning off the heat.
7. Serve immediately.
8. Adding meat to the dish is optional.

Nutritional Information

- Calories - 252
- Carbohydrates - 22g - (7%)
- Protein - 13g - (26%)
- Total Fat - 14g - (22%)
- Cholesterol - 9mg - (3%)
- Sodium - 538mg - (22%)
- Fiber - 3g - (12%)

Percent Daily Values are based on a 2000 calorie diet.

Classy Spaghetti with Spiralized Zucchini

Servings: 2-3

Ingredients

- 2-3 medium sized zucchini tightly spiralized
- 1 celery stalks finely sliced
- 1 small onion finely chopped
- 2 garlic cloves finely chopped
- 4 cups (250g) mushrooms roughly chopped
- 1 1/2 cups (200g) meat of your choice
- 2 tbsp olive oil
- 2 1/2 cups (600g) spaghetti sauce
- Salt and pepper to taste

Instructions

1. Sauté the onion, garlic in the gently heated olive oil till tender.
2. Add the celery and mushrooms and cook till soft.

3. Add the meat and cook thoroughly.
4. Add the spaghetti sauce to the cooked meat and allow to boil gently for 10 minutes, season with pepper and salt.
5. Place the spiralized zucchini into a serving bowl.
6. Add the sauce to the zucchini and serve!

Nutritional Information

- Calories - 708
- Carbohydrates - 50g - (17%)
- Protein - 39g - (78%)
- Total Fat - 41g - (63%)
- Cholesterol - 87mg - (29%)
- Sodium - 1949mg - (81%)
- Fiber - 6g - (24%)

Percent Daily Values are based on a 2000 calorie diet.

Zucchini Noodle Soup with Chicken

Servings: 4-6

Ingredients

- 1/2 fresh whole chicken
- 1 cup (240ml) chicken broth
- 3 carrots roughly chopped
- 4 celery stalks roughly chopped
- 1 onion roughly chopped
- 1 cup (60g) fresh parsley
- 3 bay leaves
- 1/2 tbsp peppercorns
- 8-10 large zucchini tightly spiralized
- Sea Salt and freshly ground pepper.

Instructions

1. Place the spiralized zucchini is a strainer and rub in the salt. Let it drain for 30 minutes.
2. Rinse out the salt and set aside.
3. Place the chicken in a pot. Sprinkle the vegetables (except zucchini) on top of the chicken.
4. Wrap the spices in a muslin bag and secure it with a string that will withstand the cooking heat and add it to the pot.
5. Add the broth and top it off with water to submerge all ingredients completely. Let it simmer for 7-8 hours.
6. Remove the chicken from the pot, debone the chicken, shred the meat and discard the bones.
7. Filter the broth to remove vegetables and the spices.
8. Season the broth with sea salt and freshly ground pepper according to taste.
9. Place the spiralized zucchini in your serving bowl.
10. Top it off with chicken broth and shredded chicken.
11. Serve immediately.

Nutritional Information

- Calories - 327
- Carbohydrates - 32g - (11%)
- Protein - 20g - (40%)
- Total Fat - 12g - (18%)
- Cholesterol - 60mg - (20%)
- Sodium - 1010mg - (42%)
- Fiber - 10g - (40%)

Percent Daily Values are based on a 2000 calorie diet.

Chapter 5 – 10 Anti-inflammatory Recipes Using Spiralized Fruits and Vegetables

Some fruits and vegetables are known to have anti inflammatory properties. You can benefit immensely from these ingredients by using them in specific recipes. Here are a few of these to get you started.

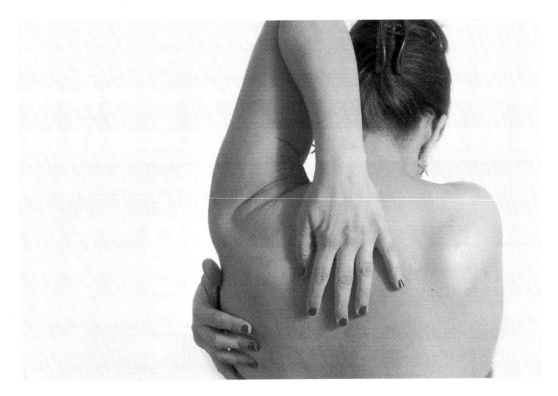

Spicy Zucchini Pasta with Garlic and Cheese

Servings: 2-3

Ingredients

- 2 large zucchini tightly spiralized
- 1 garlic clove finely chopped
- 1 tbsp organic butter
- 1-2 tsp grated goat's cheese
- 1-2 tsp red pepper flakes crushed
- Pinch of crushed Sea Salt flakes
- Freshly ground pepper

Instructions

1. Sauté the garlic and organic butter in a pan.
2. Add the zucchini and cook for 1 minute.
3. Dish out the spiralized zucchini onto your serving plate.
4. Sprinkly the grated goats cheese, crushed sea salt flakes, freshly ground pepper and red pepper flakes over the zucchini pasta.
5. Serve immediately.

Nutritional Information

- Calories - 112
- Carbohydrates - 12g - (4%)
- Protein - 4g - (8%)
- Total Fat - 7g - (11%)
- Cholesterol - 16mg - (5%)
- Sodium - 111mg - (5%)
- Fiber - 4g - (16%)

Percent Daily Values are based on a 2000 calorie diet.

Spiralized Sweet Potato with Green Curry

Servings: 4-6

Ingredients

- 2 large sweet potatoes tightly spiralized, or 4 small ones
- 1 onion finely chopped
- 3-4 garlic cloves finely chopped
- 1 tbsp ginger finely chopped
- 1 tbsp coconut oil
- 2/3 cup (160g) coconut cream
- 1 tbsp green curry paste
- 1 tsp lime zest
- 1/3 cup (40g) lightly roasted nuts almonds and/or cashews
- Salt and pepper to taste
- cilantro (coriander) for garnishing

Instructions

1. Steam the spiralized sweet potatoes for 2-3 minutes. Cool immediately and set aside.
2. Heat the coconut oil in a pan, sauté the onions, garlic and ginger till soft and fragrant.
3. Add the green curry paste and continue cooking till fragrant.
4. Add the coconut cream (without water), lime zest, salt and pepper.
5. Cook for a further 2 minutes.
6. Add the steamed sweet potatoes and mix carefully.
7. Cook for another 2-3 minutes and dish out into a serving plate.
8. Top it off with roasted nuts and garnish with the cilantro. Serve immediately.

Nutritional Information

- Calories - 344
- Carbohydrates - 21g - (7%)
- Protein - 7g - (14%)
- Total Fat - 27g - (42%)
- Sodium - 257mg - (11%)

- Fiber - 5g - (20%)

Percent Daily Values are based on a 2000 calorie diet.

Vegan Alfredo Pasta

Servings: 6-8

Ingredients

- 4-5 zucchini tightly spiralized
- 1 bell pepper sliced, 1/4 inch (1/2 cm) width
- 1/2 cup (90g) tomatoes cubed
- 1 - 1 1/2 (240ml – 360ml) cup vegetable broth
- 3 cups (540g) steamed mixed green vegetables (a mixture of spinach, chard, bok choy or any other green vegetables of your choice)
- 1 cup (120g) walnuts crushed
- 1 tsp vinegar
- 1 tbsp fresh basil leaves crushed
- 1 tsp fresh oregano
- 1 garlic clove finely chopped
- 1 tsp honey
- 1 tsp olive oil

Instructions

1. Soak the walnuts in 1 cup water and set aside.
2. Remove the stem and seeds of the bell pepper and cut it in 1 inch cubes.
3. Place the bell pepper inner side up on an oven tray lined with baking parchment paper.
4. Preheat the oven at 425 degrees and roast the bell peppers for 25 minutes.
5. Steam the green vegetables and set aside, keeping it warm.
6. Drain the walnuts. Add them to a pan together with the roasted bell pepper, tomatoes and vegetable broth.
7. Puree the ingredients in the pan using a stick blender.
8. Add vinegar, basil, oregano, garlic, honey and heat the mixture slightly.

9. In another pan, sauté the spiralized zucchini with olive oil until tender (about 4 minutes).
10. Pour the mixture over the spiralized zucchini and mix carefully till the zucchini is coated with the mixture.
11. Serve immediately with the steamed green vegetables.

Nutritional Information

- Calories - 207
- Carbohydrates - 14g - (5%)
- Protein - 7g - (14%)
- Total Fat - 16g - (25%)
- Sodium - 466mg - (19%)
- Fiber - 5g - (20%)

Percent Daily Values are based on a 2000 calorie diet.

Spicy Cabbage Noodles with Beef

Servings: 6-8

Ingredients

- 1 cabbage tightly spiralized
- 7 cups (900g) minced meat grass fed beef or chicken
- 2 tsp coconut oil for cooking
- 5-6 tbsp almond butter
- 2 tbsp apple cider vinegar
- 2 tbsp ground desiccated coconut
- 1 tbsp sesame oil
- 2 tbsp hot sauce of your choice
- 1-2 tbsp stevia syrup

Instructions

1. In a bowl, mix together almond butter, vinegar, ground desiccated coconut, sesame oil, hot sauce and stevia. Leave aside for later.

2. Heat the coconut oil in a pan.
3. Add the meat and cook thoroughly.
4. Add the cabbage when the meat is cooked; cover the pan and cook for 10 minutes or shorter if a slightly crunchy texture is preferred.
5. Dish out into a serving dish, pour the sauce over the beef and cabbage.
6. Mix thoroughly and serve.

Nutritional Information

- Calories - 582
- Carbohydrates - 12g - (4%)
- Protein - 43g - (86%)
- Total Fat - 41g - (63%)
- Cholesterol - 134mg - (45%)
- Sodium - 810mg - (34%)
- Fiber - 5g - (20%)

Percent Daily Values are based on a 2000 calorie diet.

Spiralized Eggplant with Cheese

Servings: 1

Ingredients

- 1 eggplant tightly spiralized
- 1/2 cup (50g) Parmesan cheese or manchego vieja, a hard cheese made from goat's milk
- 1 - 1 1/2 cup (250-375g) marinara sauce
- 1dessert spoon olive oil
- Sea Salt and freshly ground black pepper to taste

Instructions

1. Spiralize the eggplant and let it sit in salted water for 15-20 minutes. Drain the water.

2. Heat the olive oil in a pan, ensuring that the heat is turned down low so as not to burn the olive oil.
3. Add the eggplant noodles and cook until soft over low heat. Toss continuously to ensure thorough cooking.
4. Add the marinara sauce and add the salt and pepper according to taste.
5. Sprinkle the eggplant generously with the grated cheese and serve immediately.

Nutritional Information

- Calories - 629
- Carbohydrates - 61g - (20%)
- Protein - 30g - (60%)
- Total Fat - 32g - (49%)
- Cholesterol - 44mg - (15%)
- Sodium - 2133mg - (89%)
- Fiber - 20g - (80%)

Percent Daily Values are based on a 2000 calorie diet.

Red and Orange Salad

Servings: 4-6

Ingredients

- 2 large sweet potatoes tightly spiralized
- 3-4 beets tightly spiralized
- 4 green onion stalks cut into 1/2 inch slices
- 1/2 cup (60g) pumpkin seeds toasted

For Dressing:

- 1/3 cup (80ml) olive oil
- 1/4 cup (50ml) lemon juice
- 1 tsp lemon zest
- 1 garlic clove finely chopped

- 2 tbsp raw organic honey
- 2 tbsp organic cream
- Sea Salt and freshly ground pepper to taste

Instructions Dressing:

1. Mix all the ingredients for the dressing in a bowl.
2. Place in an airtight container and set aside for later.

Making up the Salad:

1. Place all the salad ingredients and the dressing in a bowl and mix carefully, taking care not to break the spiralized vegetables.
2. Serve immediately.

Nutritional Information

- Calories - 388
- Carbohydrates - 28g - (9%)
- Protein - 7g - (14%)
- Total Fat - 29g - (45%)
- Cholesterol - 10mg - (3%)
- Sodium - 137mg - (6%)
- Fiber - 4g - (16%)

Percent Daily Values are based on a 2000 calorie diet.

Spiralized Beet and Avocado Salad with Vinaigrette

Servings: 2

Ingredients

Ingredients for cooking:

- 4 beets tightly spiralized
- 1 blood orange juiced

- 1 tbsp olive oil
- Pinch of sea salt and freshly ground black pepper

Uncooked ingredients:

- 1 avocado cubed
- 2 lettuce leaves cleaned and shredded
- 2 blood oranges skinned and segmented
- 1 tbsp chives chopped roughly

Ingredients for roasting:

- 3 tbsp almond flakes
- 1 tbsp pumpkin seeds

Ingredients for the Vinaigrette:

- 1/2 cup (120ml) blood orange juice
- 1 lemon; juice from the whole lemon
- 1 tbsp vinegar
- 5-6 tbsp extra virgin olive oil
- 2 tsp raw honey
- Sea Salt and freshly ground black pepper to taste

Instructions

For the Vinaigrette:

1. Mix all the ingredients thoroughly in a bowl. Place in an airtight container and set aside for later.

For the Salad:

1. Make a pouch using aluminum foil, which has been lined with baking parchment. Place the beet spirals in it along with blood orange juice, olive oil, salt and pepper. Seal it tightly and bake till the beet cooked. Set aside to cool.

2. Place the almond flakes and pumpkin seeds on a baking tray and roast, roast under low heat till golden brown, taking care not to burn the almond flakes and pumpkin seeds.
3. Set aside to cool. When cooled, place in an airtight container to maintain the crispness.
4. Place the shredded lettuce, cubed avocado, segmented blood orange, cooked beet and dressing in a bowl and mix thoroughly.
5. Sprinkle the roasted almond and pumpkin seeds on the top of the salad and serve.

Nutritional Information

- Calories - 888
- Carbohydrates - 64g - (21%)
- Protein - 13g - (26%)
- Total Fat - 69g - (106%)
- Sodium - 382mg - (16%)
- Fiber - 18g - (72%)

Percent Daily Values are based on a 2000 calorie diet.

Spiralized Butternut Squash Pasta

Servings: 4-6

Ingredients

- 1 large butternut squash tightly spiralized
- 2 bell peppers
- 1/2 tsp garlic powder
- 2 garlic cloves finely chopped
- 1/4 tsp red pepper flakes
- 2-3 small onions cubed
- 1/3 (80ml) cup chicken broth
- 1 cup (135g) chicken cooked and cubed
- 1 tbsp roughly chopped parsley
- olive oil
- Salt and black pepper to taste

Instructions

1. Remove the stem and seeds of the bell peppers and cut them into 1 inch cubes. Place them on the baking tray with their inner sides up. Roast for 20 to 25 minutes. When cooled, puree the roasted bell peppers in a blender.
2. On another baking tray, place the spiralized butternut squash. Season it with olive oil, salt, pepper and garlic powder. Roast for 10 minutes. Transfer it to your serving bowls.
3. Heat some olive oil in a pan. Add finely chopped garlic, red pepper flakes, and onions. Cook thoroughly and add the pureed bell peppers.
4. Add the chicken broth and chicken. Cook for 2 to 5 minutes.
5. Pour this mixture over the spiralized butternut squash.
6. Top it off with parsley and enjoy!

Nutritional Information

- Calories - 249
- Carbohydrates - 35g - (12%)
- Protein - 13g - (26%)
- Total Fat - 9g - (14%)
- Cholesterol - 29mg - (10%)
- Sodium - 251mg - (10%)
- Fiber - 6g - (24%)

Percent Daily Values are based on a 2000 calorie diet.

Spiralized Sweet Potato with Avocado Soup

Servings: 4-6

Ingredients

- 1 large sweet potato tightly spiralized
- 1 avocado cubed
- 3 cups (720ml) vegetable broth
- 1 small onion chopped
- 1 garlic clove finely chopped

- 3 cups (400g) tomatoes diced
- 1/2 tsp cumin seeds
- 1 tbsp chili powder
- 1 tbsp olive oil
- 1-2 tbsp cilantro
- Salt and black pepper to taste

Instructions

1. Heat olive oil in a pan. Add garlic and cook for 1 minute.
2. Add the onions and cook for 2-3 minutes until tender.
3. Next add the tomatoes, cumin, chili powder, salt and pepper and cook for 5-6 minutes.
4. Add the chicken broth and bring it to a boil.
5. Add the sweet potato spirals and cook. Add the cilantro and avocado.
6. Dish out into a serving dish and serve immediately.

Nutritional Information

- Calories - 208
- Carbohydrates - 23g - (8%)
- Protein - 3g - (6%)
- Total Fat - 13g - (20%)
- Sodium - 523mg - (22%)
- Fiber - 7g - (28%)

Percent Daily Values are based on a 2000 calorie diet.

Kale and Beetroot Salad with Goat Cheese

Servings: 4-6

Ingredients

- 4 cups (270g) kale leaves roughly chopped
- 1 beet tightly spiralized
- 1 apple tightly spiralized

- 1 cup (170g) quinoa seeds
- 1/4 cup (30g) walnuts toasted
- 1/4 cup (30g) cranberries dried
- 1 cup (140g) goat cheese crumbled
- 2 green onions finely chopped
- 1/2 tbsp lemon juice
- 1/2 tbsp olive oil
- Salt and black pepper to taste

For Sauce:

- 2 tbsp flaxseed oil
- 2 tbsp olive oil
- 1 tbsp honey
- 1/4 cup (60ml) apple cider vinegar
- 1 tsp mustard paste
- 1 tsp horseradish paste
- 1 garlic clove finely chopped
- Salt and black pepper to taste

Instructions

For the Sauce:

1. Mix all the ingredients carefully in a bowl.
2. Place in an airtight container for storage.

For the Salad:

1. Place quinoa in a pan with 2 cups water.
2. Cook for 15-20 minutes until the quinoa absorbs water.
3. Add the sauce and remove from the heat.
4. Mix the remaining ingredients in a bowl.
5. Add the quinoa mixture to the ingredients. Toss and serve.

Nutritional Information

- Calories - 557

- Carbohydrates - 55g - (18%)
- Protein - 17g - (34%)
- Total Fat - 32g - (49%)
- Cholesterol - 24mg - (8%)
- Sodium - 267mg - (11%)
- Fiber - 6g - (24%)

Percent Daily Values are based on a 2000 calorie diet.

Chapter 6 – 10 Spiralized Recipes to Promote Heart Health

Some fruits and vegetables are known to promote heart health. Include more of these ingredients in your daily diet through the following recipes.

Sweet and Sour Zucchini Salad

Servings: 2-3

Ingredients

- 1 zucchini tightly spiralized
- 1/2 cup (100g) mixed vegetables (diced peppers, carrots, garden peas)
- 1/2 cup (110g) cottage cheese cubed and slightly toasted

For Dressing:

- 1/4 cup (50g) mayonnaise
- 3 tbsp honey
- 1-2 tbsp lemon juice
- 1 tsp extra virgin olive oil
- 1 tsp basil
- 1/2 tsp dill finely chopped
- Salt and black pepper to taste

Instructions

For Dressing:

1. Mix all the ingredients carefully in a bowl. Keep aside.

For Salad:

1. Mix all the ingredients with the dressing; marinate for 30 minutes.
2. Dish out into a serving bowl and serve.

Nutritional Information

- Calories - 410
- Carbohydrates - 37g - (12%)
- Protein - 10g - (20%)
- Total Fat - 26g - (40%)
- Cholesterol - 19mg - (6%)
- Sodium - 614mg - (26%)

- Fiber - 3g - (12%)

Percent Daily Values are based on a 2000 calorie diet.

Zucchini Pasta with Lemon and Almond Paste

Servings: 2

Ingredients

- 2-3 zucchini tightly spiralized

For Dressing:

- 1 cup (110g) almonds roasted and crushed
- 1 tbsp lemon zest
- 1 tbsp basil
- 1/2 tsp garlic paste
- 1/4 tsp red pepper flakes
- 1/2 cup (120ml) extra virgin olive oil
- 1 tbsp lemon juice
- Salt and pepper to taste

Instructions

For Dressing:

1. Add all the dry ingredients to the blender and blend.
2. While the blender is running on low speed, add extra virgin olive oil slowly.
3. Add the lemon juice at the end.
4. Pour into a container and set aside.

For the Pasta:

1. Place spiralized zucchini in a bowl.
2. Pour the dressing over the Zucchini and mix well.
3. Dish out into a serving dish. Serve chilled.

Nutritional Information

- Calories - 825
- Carbohydrates - 19g - (6%)
- Protein - 14g - (28%)
- Total Fat - 82g - (126%)
- Sodium - 98mg - (4%)
- Fiber - 9g - (36%)

Percent Daily Values are based on a 2000 calorie diet.

Spiralized Zucchini Pasta with Capers and Olives

Servings: 2-4

Ingredients

- 4-5 medium sized zucchini tightly spiralized
- 1 garlic clove minced
- 12-15 olives pitted and sliced
- 1 tbsp capers
- 1/4 tsp red pepper flakes
- 1 tbsp basil leaves crushed
- 2 tbsp extra virgin olive oil
- 1 tbsp lemon juice
- Salt and black pepper to taste

Instructions

1. Place the garlic, capers, olives, salt and red pepper flakes on the chopping board. Using the chef's knife on the side, mix these ingredients to a paste-like consistency.
2. Shift to a bowl and add olive oil, tomatoes and basil.
3. Let it marinate for 15-20 minutes.
4. Add the spiralized zucchini to this mixture. Toss and serve.

Nutritional Information

- Calories - 128
- Carbohydrates - 16g - (5%)
- Protein - 5g - (10%)
- Total Fat - 7g - (11%)
- Sodium - 504mg - (21%)
- Fiber - 5g - (20%)

Percent Daily Values are based on a 2000 calorie diet.

Tangy Zucchini Pasta with Tomatoes and Artichoke

Servings: 4

Ingredients

- 4 zucchini tightly spiralized
- 1 cup (150g) cherry tomatoes sliced in half
- 1 cup (160g) artichoke sliced in half
- 1 tsp lemon zest
- 2-3 tbsp lemon juice
- 1-2 tbsp vinegar
- 3 garlic cloves finely chopped
- 2-3 tbsp grapeseed oil
- 2 tbsp parsley roughly chopped
- 1/2 cup (70g) goat cheese crumbled
- Salt and black pepper to taste

Instructions

1. Mix parsley, garlic, vinegar, lemon juice, lemon zest and grapeseed oil in a bowl.
2. Add the remaining ingredients to this mixture. Toss thoroughly and serve.

Nutritional Information

- Calories - 188
- Carbohydrates - 15g - (5%)
- Protein - 9g - (18%)
- Total Fat - 13g - (20%)
- Cholesterol - 14mg - (5%)
- Sodium - 273mg - (11%)
- Fiber - 5g - (20%)

Percent Daily Values are based on a 2000 calorie diet.

Simply Sweet Potato

Servings: 3-4

Ingredients

- 2 large sweet potatoes tightly spiralized
- 2 tbsp olive oil
- 2 tsp garlic paste
- 1/4 tsp red pepper flakes
- 1/2 cup (50g) onion diced
- 1 cup (135g) cubed meat
- 2 eggs
- 1/2 cup (50g) Parmesan cheese grated
- Salt and pepper to taste

Instructions

For the Sauce:

1. Whisk the eggs and parmesan cheese in a bowl and season with salt and pepper. Set aside.

For the Sweet Potato:

1. Heat a grill pan and coat it with non-stick cooking spray.
2. Sauté the spiralized sweet potatoes on medium heat until tender.
3. In another pan, heat the olive oil. Add garlic and red chili flakes and cook for about 1 minute.
4. Add the onions. Cook until the onions turn translucent.
5. Add the meat and cook thoroughly.
6. Add the sweet potato spirals to this mixture and toss thoroughly.
7. Now add the sauce slowly while mixing continuously.
8. Transfer to the serving bowls and enjoy!

Nutritional Information

- Calories - 395
- Carbohydrates - 18g - (6%)
- Protein - 23g - (46%)
- Total Fat - 25g - (38%)
- Cholesterol - 178mg - (59%)
- Sodium - 558mg - (23%)
- Fiber - 2g - (8%)

Percent Daily Values are based on a 2000 calorie diet.

Zucchini and Corn with Vinaigrette

Servings: 4

Ingredients

- 4-5 medium sized zucchini tightly spiralized
- 2 cups (500g) of corns removed from the cob
- 1 cup (150g) cherry tomatoes sliced in half
- 1/2 cup (20g) basil leaves roughly chopped
- 1/2 cup (50g) Parmesan cheese grated

For the Vinaigrette:

- 1/4 cup (60ml) vinegar
- 1/4 cup (60ml) olive oil
- 1/4 cup (60ml) grapeseed oil
- 1 garlic clove finely chopped
- 1/4 tsp sugar
- Salt and black pepper to taste

Instructions

For Vinaigrette:

1. Mix all the ingredients thoroughly in a bowl. Use an airtight glass bottle to store this mixture.

For the Recipe:

1. Mix the zucchini, corn and tomatoes in a serving bowl.
2. Add a generous amount of the vinaigrette.
3. Place the basil leaves and sprinkle the parmesan cheese over the top and serve!

Nutritional Information

- Calories - 403
- Carbohydrates - 24g - (8%)
- Protein - 10g - (20%)
- Total Fat - 32g - (49%)
- Cholesterol - 11mg - (4%)
- Sodium - 263mg - (11%)
- Fiber - 5g - (20%)

Percent Daily Values are based on a 2000 calorie diet.

Spiralized Celeriac and Chickpea Soup

Servings: 4-6

Ingredients

- 1 medium celeriac tightly spiralized
- 2-3 carrots tightly spiralized
- 1 onion finely chopped
- 2-3 garlic cloves finely chopped
- 1 1/2 cups (360g) chickpeas cooked and drained
- 1 tbsp olive oil
- 1 vegetable stock cube
- 1 tsp dried thyme
- 1/2 tsp paprika powder
- 1/2 tsp turmeric powder
- 1/4 tsp rosemary powder
- 1/4 cup (50g) cheese parmesan or cottage
- Salt and pepper to taste

Instructions

1. Heat the olive oil in a pan. Add the onions and cook till fragrant and translucent.
2. Add garlic and sauté for another 2-3 minutes.
3. Add 5 cups of water, chickpeas, thyme, vegetable stock, paprika, turmeric and rosemary and bring this mixture to a boil.
4. Now add the celeriac and carrots and cook for 12-15 minutes.
5. Season with salt and pepper to taste.
6. Dish into a serving bowl, sprinkle with cheese and serve!

Nutritional Information

- Calories - 208
- Carbohydrates - 30g - (10%)
- Protein - 8g - (16%)
- Total Fat - 7g - (11%)
- Cholesterol - 6mg - (2%)

- Sodium - 385mg - (16%)
- Fiber - 6g - (24%)

Percent Daily Values are based on a 2000 calorie diet.

Zucchini and Summer Squash Pasta

Servings: 4-6

Ingredients

- 2 medium sized zucchini tightly spiralized
- 2 medium sized summer squash tightly spiralized
- 1/4 cup (60ml) chicken or vegetable broth
- 4-5 garlic cloves finely chopped
- 1/2 tsp thyme dried
- Salt and black pepper to taste

Instructions

1. In a pan, heat the chicken broth and garlic.
2. Add the zucchini, summer squash, thyme, salt and pepper and cook until tender. Dish out and serve immediately!

Nutritional Information

- Calories - 38
- Carbohydrates - 8g - (3%)
- Protein - 3g - (6%)
- Total Fat - 0.5g - (1%)
- Sodium - 100mg - (4%)
- Fiber - 2g - (8%)

Percent Daily Values are based on a 2000 calorie diet.

Carrot and Zucchini Pasta with Green Sauce

Servings: 4-6

Ingredients

- 2 carrots tightly spiralized
- 2 zucchini tightly spiralized
- 3 cups (90g) baby spinach washed and roughly chopped
- 1/4 cup (30g) pumpkin seeds
- 2-3 garlic cloves chopped
- 2-3 tbsp olive oil
- Salt and black pepper to taste

Instructions

1. Place the spiralized zucchini and carrots in a bowl.
2. Add the remaining ingredients to the blender and blend to a saucy consistency.
3. Add this sauce to the vegetables, toss and serve.

Nutritional Information

- Calories - 142
- Carbohydrates - 8g - (3%)
- Protein - 5g - (10%)
- Total Fat - 11g - (17%)
- Sodium - 97mg - (4%)
- Fiber - 3g - (12%)

Percent Daily Values are based on a 2000 calorie diet.

Spiralized Jicama Fried

Servings: 2-4

Ingredients

- 1 jicama spiralized to resemble curly fries
- 1 tbsp onion powder
- 1-2 tsp cayenne pepper
- 1-2 tsp chili powder
- 1-2 tbsp olive oil
- salt as required

Instructions

1. Place the spiralized jicama in a bowl.
2. Add the remaining ingredients and toss thoroughly to coat evenly.
3. Transfer it to a baking tray. Preheat the oven at 405 degrees and bake the jicama fried for 10-15 minutes.
4. Turn over the fries and bake again for 10-15 minutes or until well-done. Serve immediately.

Nutritional Information

- Calories - 204
- Carbohydrates - 33g - (11%)
- Protein - 3g - (6%)
- Total Fat - 7g - (11%)
- Sodium - 106mg - (4%)
- Fiber - 17g - (68%)

Percent Daily Values are based on a 2000 calorie diet.

Chapter 7 – 10 Anti-Aging Spiralized Salad Recipes

Would you like to remain young and vibrant forever? The foods you consume play an important role in promoting health and longevity. Here are a few anti-aging recipes to help you achieve timelessness.

Spiralized Sweet Potato with Brussels Sprouts

Servings: 2-4

Ingredients

- 1 sweet potato tightly spiralized
- 6 cups (500g) of Brussels sprouts cut into quarters
- 2 tbsp grapeseed oil
- 2 tbsp maple syrup
- 1 tsp garlic powder
- 1 cup (125g) pistachios
- salt as required

Instructions

1. Spiralize the sweet potato and set aside.
2. In a pan, add the oil, maple syrup and Brussels sprouts.
3. Cook on low heat until soft.
4. Add the sweet potato spirals with a pinch of salt and cook for another 2-3 minutes.
5. Add the pistachios and remove from flame.
6. Serve immediately!

Nutritional Information

- Calories - 683
- Carbohydrates - 67g - (22%)
- Protein - 22g - (44%)
- Total Fat - 42g - (65%)
- Sodium - 101mg - (4%)
- Fiber - 18g - (72%)

Percent Daily Values are based on a 2000 calorie diet.

Carrot and Apple Salad with Brussels Sprouts

Servings: 4-6

Ingredients

- 1-2 carrots tightly spiralized
- 1 apple tightly spiralized
- 6 cups (500g) Brussels sprouts cut into quarters
- 1/2 cup (55g) cranberries dried and diced
- 1/2 cup (50g) almonds crushed

For Dressing:

- 3-4 tbsp lemon juice
- 2 tbsp grapeseed oil
- 1-2 tbsp honey
- salt as required

Instructions

For the Dressing:

1. Mix the ingredients carefully in a bowl. Set aside.

For the Salad:

1. Place all the remaining ingredients in a bowl.
2. Add a generous amount of the dressing.
3. Toss and leave for 30 minutes to marinate. Serve chilled.

Nutritional Information

- Calories - 281
- Carbohydrates - 38g - (13%)
- Protein - 8g - (16%)
- Total Fat - 15g - (23%)
- Sodium - 47mg - (2%)
- Fiber - 9g - (36%)

Percent Daily Values are based on a 2000 calorie diet.

Brussels Sprouts and Carrots in Ginger and Garlic Dressing

Servings: 4-6

Ingredients

- 6 cups (500g) of Brussels sprouts cut into quarters
- 1 large carrot tightly spiralized
- 1/2 cup (50g) pecans

For the Dressing:

- 1/2 cup (120ml) orange juice freshly squeezed
- 2 tbsp grapeseed oil
- 2 tbsp apple cider vinegar
- 1 garlic clove finely chopped
- 1 tsp ginger finely chopped
- salt as required

Instructions

For the Dressing:

1. Combine all the ingredients carefully in a bowl. Set aside.

For the Salad:

1. Place the remaining ingredients in a bowl.
2. Add the dressing and toss to coat evenly.
3. Leave it to marinate for 2-3 days and serve chilled.

Nutritional Information

- Calories - 226
- Carbohydrates - 19g - (6%)
- Protein - 6g - (12%)
- Total Fat - 17g - (26%)
- Sodium - 46mg - (2%)
- Fiber - 7g - (28%)

Percent Daily Values are based on a 2000 calorie diet.

Cooked Vegetable Salad

Servings: 4-6

Ingredients

- 2 sweet potatoes tightly spiralized
- 3 small carrots tightly spiralized
- 1 bell pepper spiralized
- 1 onion finely chopped
- 1 1/2 cups (100g) mushrooms sliced
- 7-8 kale leaves stem removed and roughly chopped
- 2-3 green onions roughly chopped
- 1/3 cup (80ml) soy sauce
- 1 tbsp maple syrup
- 1 tbsp sesame oil

Instructions

1. Mix the soy sauce, maple syrup and 1 tbsp sesame oil in a bowl. Set aside.
2. In a pan, add the sesame oil and the spiralized sweet potato. Cook until tender.
3. Add in the soy sauce mixture and cook for 2-3 minutes.
4. Dish out on the serving plates.
5. In another pan, add 2 tbsp sesame oil and the onion.
6. Cook until the onion turns transparent.
7. Add the remaining ingredients and toss thoroughly to cook.
8. Add these vegetables on top of the sweet potato spirals.
9. Garnish with green onions and serve.

Nutritional Information

- Calories - 170
- Carbohydrates - 31g - (10%)
- Protein - 5g - (10%)
- Total Fat - 4g - (6%)
- Sodium - 1278mg - (53%)
- Fiber - 5g - (20%)

Percent Daily Values are based on a 2000 calorie diet.

Zucchini and Apple Salad

Servings: 4-6

Ingredients

- 2 medium sized zucchini spiralized
- 1 green apple spiralized
- 4 cups (120g) spinach leaves roughly chopped
- 4 cups (270g) kale leaves roughly chopped
- 1-2 tbsp vinegar
- 1-2 tbsp olive oil
- 1-2 tbsp maple syrup
- Salt as required

Instructions

1. Mix the vinegar, olive oil, maple syrup and salt in a bowl. Set aside.
2. Add the remaining ingredients into a serving bowl.
3. Pour the dressing and toss to coat evenly. Serve chilled.

Nutritional Information

- Calories - 118
- Carbohydrates - 19g - (6%)
- Protein - 4g - (8%)
- Total Fat - 4g - (6%)
- Sodium - 64mg - (3%)
- Fiber - 4g - (16%)

Percent Daily Values are based on a 2000 calorie diet.

Vegan Alfredo with Spiralized Sweet Potato

Servings: 4-6

Ingredients

- 2 sweet potatos tightly spiralized
- 1/2 cup (125g) pumpkin puree
- 1 1/2 cup (150g) cashew nuts
- 2 tbsp lemon juice
- 2 garlic cloves finely chopped
- 1 tsp parsley
- 1/4 tsp nutmeg powder
- Salt and black pepper to taste

Instructions

1. Add all the ingredients except sweet potatoes to a blender and blend to the desired consistency.
2. Place the spiralized sweet potatoes in your serving bowl.
3. Top it off with generous amounts of the sauce and serve.

Nutritional Information

- Calories - 294
- Carbohydrates - 28g - (9%)
- Protein - 9g - (18%)
- Total Fat - 18g - (28%)
- Cholesterol - 1mg - (0%)
- Sodium - 267mg - (11%)
- Fiber - 4g - (16%)

Percent Daily Values are based on a 2000 calorie diet.

Sweet and Tangy Asparagus and Cabbage Salad

Servings: 6-8

Ingredients

- 4 cups (500g) asparagus trimmed and sliced length-wise
- 1 cup (70g) cabbage spiralized
- 1 apple spiralized
- 3 tbsp mint leaves roughly chopped
- 3 green onions roughly chopped
- 1/2 cup (75g) peanuts toasted and crushed

For the Dressing:

- 1 garlic clove finely chopped
- 1 tsp ginger finely chopped
- 1 tbsp lemon juice
- 1 tsp lemon zest
- 2 tsp chili paste
- 1 tbsp honey
- 1 tbsp vinegar
- 1 tsp sesame oil
- 2 tbsp olive oil
- Salt and black pepper to taste

Instructions

For the Dressing:

1. Mix all the ingredients carefully in a bowl. Set aside.

For the Salad:

1. Place all the remaining ingredients in a bowl.
2. Add a generous amount of the dressing.
3. Toss and serve.

Nutritional Information

- Calories - 205
- Carbohydrates - 22g - (7%)
- Protein - 8g - (16%)
- Total Fat - 12g - (18%)
- Cholesterol - 1mg - (0%)
- Sodium - 72mg - (3%)
- Fiber - 7g - (28%)

Percent Daily Values are based on a 2000 calorie diet.

Spiralized Zucchini and Sweet Potato Pasta

Servings: 6-8

Ingredients

- 2 medium sized zucchini tightly spiralized
- 2 sweet potato tightly spiralized
- 4 cups (500g) of asparagus trimmed and sliced length-wise
- 2/3 cup (100g) of grated goats cheese of your choice
- 1/2 cup (120ml) vegetable broth
- Salt as required

Instructions

1. Place the spiralized zucchini, sweet potato and asparagus trimmings on a baking tray. Sprinkle some salt and let it bake for 30-35 minutes on 350 degrees.
2. In a pan, mix the remaining ingredients and cook to a desired consistency.
3. Remove from heat and add to the vegetables.
4. Toss to coat evenly, sprinkle the grated goats cheese and serve.

Nutritional Information

- Calories - 123

- Carbohydrates - 15g - (5%)
- Protein - 7g - (14%)
- Total Fat - 5g - (8%)
- Cholesterol - 12mg - (4%)
- Sodium - 144mg - (6%)
- Fiber - 4g - (16%)

Percent Daily Values are based on a 2000 calorie diet.

Green Zucchini Pasta with Shrimps

Servings: 3-4

Ingredients

- 2lb (1kg) cooked shrimps.
- 4 large zucchini tightly spiralized
- 4 cups (500g) asparagus end trimmed and sliced length-wise
- Extra virgin olive oil and black pepper for garnishing

For the Green Sauce:

- 3 garlic cloves finely chopped
- 1-2 cups (34-68g) of watercress roughly chopped
- 1 cup (25g) mint leaves roughly chopped
- 1/2 cup (30g) parsley roughly chopped
- 1/2 cup (120ml) tahini sauce
- 2-3 tbsp lemon juice
- 1/4 tsp red pepper flakes
- 2 tbsp extra virgin olive oil
- Salt as required

Instructions

For the Green Sauce:

1. Add all the ingredients to the blender and blend to a smooth consistency. Set aside.

For the Salad:

1. Cook the spiralized zucchini in water with some salt for a couple of minutes. Transfer to an ice bath to cool.
2. Repeat the procedure with asparagus.
3. Place all the zucchini, asparagus and shrimps into a serving bowl. Add the green sauce and toss.
4. Serve immediately.

Nutritional Information

- Calories - 647
- Carbohydrates - 28g - (9%)
- Protein - 79g - (158%)
- Total Fat - 25g - (38%)
- Cholesterol - 590mg - (197%)
- Sodium - 871mg - (36%)
- Fiber - 12g - (48%)

Percent Daily Values are based on a 2000 calorie diet.

Spiralized Rutabaga Bolognaise

Servings: 4-6

Ingredients

- 4-6 rutabaga tightly spiralized
- 2 onions finely chopped
- 2 celery stalks sliced
- 3 garlic cloves finely chopped
- 3-4 cups (400-550g) chicken cubed
- 1-2 cups (240- 475ml) chicken broth
- 15 large tomatoes peeled and cubed

- 1 tsp chili powder
- 1 tbsp garlic powder
- 1/2 tsp white pepper
- 3 tbsp oregano
- 2 tbsp thyme
- 4 tbsp parsley
- 1 tsp cinnamon
- 1/4 tsp clove powder
- 2-3 bay leaves
- Salt as required

Instructions

1. Heat the coconut oil in a pan on a high flame.
2. Place the chicken cubes on the skillet and cook till the chicken turns golden brown on all sides.
3. Dish out on a plate and set aside.
4. Add a little more coconut oil in the same pan, add the onions, celery and garlic with some coconut oil and cook on medium flame for 2-3 minutes.
5. Add the cooked chicken cubes, tomato cubes and the seasonings.
6. Add the chicken broth and simmer on low heat for 2-3 hours till all the ingredients are cooked thoroughly.
7. Steam the spiralized rutabaga for 4-5 minutes or until well-cooked.
8. Place the rutabaga on your serving plate.
9. Pour the chicken and tomato sauce over the rutabaga and serve immediately!

Nutritional Information

- Calories - 450
- Carbohydrates - 45g - (15%)
- Protein - 35g - (70%)
- Total Fat - 16g - (25%)
- Cholesterol - 88mg - (29%)
- Sodium - 705mg - (29%)
- Fiber - 14g - (56%)

Percent Daily Values are based on a 2000 calorie diet.

Chapter 8 – 10 Spiralized Recipes for Radiant Skin

Your skin says a lot about your health! Here are some of the recipes you can use to get clear and radiant skin.

Zucchini Pasta with a Twist

Servings: 6-8

Ingredients

- 7-8 medium sized zucchini tightly spiralized
- 1 bell pepper tightly spiralized
- 1/2 cup (35g) mushrooms sliced
- 4 cups (500g) asparagus trimmed and sliced

For Sauce:

- 2 tbsp tahini paste
- 1 tbsp olive oil
- 1 cup walnuts soaked in water
- 2 cups of cilantro (coriander) leaves
- 1/2 cup basil
- 1/2 tsp garlic paste
- 1/2 tsp lemon juice
- Salt and black pepper to taste

Instructions

1. Mix all the ingredients in a blender and blend till a smooth consistency is achieved. Set aside.
1. Place all the vegetables in a bowl.
2. Add the sauce and toss to cover evenly. Serve chilled.

Nutritional Information

- Calories - 218
- Carbohydrates - 16g - (5%)
- Protein - 9g - (18%)
- Total Fat - 16g - (25%)
- Sodium - 30mg - (1%)
- Fiber - 7g - (28%)

Percent Daily Values are based on a 2000 calorie diet.

Pesto Zucchini Pasta

Servings: 1

Ingredients

- 2 zucchini loosely spiralized
- 1 1/2 cups (200 g) red and yellow cherry tomatoes sliced in halves.
- 1 tbsp basil leaves whole
- 1/4 onion chopped
- 1 garlic clove finely chopped
- 2 tbsp green pesto
- 1 tbsp olive oil
- A pinch of sea salt flakes and freshly ground black pepper.
- 1/4 cup (25g) grated parmesan cheese
- 1 egg

For the pesto:

- 2 1/2 tbsp (20 g) pine nuts
- 2 cloves garlic
- 3 1/2 tbsp (50ml) virgin olive oil
- 1/2 cup (50 g) fresh basil leaves
- 1/3 cup (30 g) Parmesan cheese

Instructions

For the pesto:

1. Roast the pine nuts.
2. When the pine nuts have cooled, place in a blender with all the other ingredients for the pesto and blend.
3. Store in a container for later.

For the main dish

1. Heat some olive oil gently in a pan, add the chopped garlic and onion.

2. Saute till fragrant. Add the spiralised zucchini and cherry tomatoes and cook for 2-3 minutes.
3. Season with crushed sea salt flakes and freshly ground pepper.
4. Dish into a serving plate, add the pesto and mix thoroughly and keep warm.
5. Break the egg in the frying pan and cook for 1-2 minutes.
6. Sprinkle the grated parmesan cheese on the zucchini, garnish with the basil leaves, place the cooked egg on top and serve immediately.

Nutritional Information

- Calories - 1234
- Carbohydrates - 35g - (12%)
- Protein - 40g - (80%)
- Total Fat - 110g - (169%)
- Cholesterol - 239mg - (80%)
- Sodium - 1321mg - (55%)
- Fiber - 10g - (40%)

Percent Daily Values are based on a 2000 calorie diet.

Cucumber Mint Salad

Servings: 2-3

Ingredients

- 1 cucumber spiralized
- 1/2 cup (15g) mint leaves
- 1 green onion sliced
- 2 tbsp sesame seeds

For the Dressing:

- 2 tbsp olive oil
- 1 tbsp grapeseed oil
- 5 tbsp lemon juice
- 1 tsp soy sauce

- 1/2 tsp ginger finely chopped
- 1/2 tsp red chili flakes
- Black pepper as required

Instructions

For the Dressing:

1. Mix all the ingredients carefully in a bowl. Set aside.

For the Salad:

1. Place all the remaining ingredients in a bowl. Add the dressing, toss thoroughly and serve.

Nutritional Information

- Calories - 274
- Carbohydrates - 13g - (4%)
- Protein - 3g - (6%)
- Total Fat - 25g - (38%)
- Sodium - 163mg - (7%)
- Fiber - 3g - (12%)

Percent Daily Values are based on a 2000 calorie diet.

Zucchini and Carrot Pasta

Servings: 4-6

Ingredients

- 5 zucchini tightly spiralized
- 2-3 carrots spiralized
- 1lb (500g) organic sausages cubed
- 5 cups (800g) tomatoes peeled and cubed
- 2 cups (500g) tomato paste

- 2 onions cubed
- 2 cups (200g) celery sliced
- 3 garlic cloves finely chopped
- 1 tsp basil leaves crushed
- 1 tsp thyme
- 1 tsp oregano
- 1/2 tsp red pepper flakes
- Salt and black pepper to taste

Instructions

1. Cook the sausages as mentioned on the pack. Cut it into cubes and set aside.
2. In a pan, add some oil, onions, celery, and garlic. Cook for 8-10 minutes.
3. Add the sausages and cook for another 2-3 minutes before adding tomatoes (both paste and cubes).
4. Finally add the seasoning and let it cook for 45 minutes or until the sauce has thickened as desired.
5. Adjust the seasoning according to taste.
6. Steam the spiralized zucchini and carrots until tender.
7. Place these in your serving bowl and top off with tomato sauce and serve!

Nutritional Information

- Calories - 516
- Carbohydrates - 54g - (18%)
- Protein - 30g - (60%)
- Total Fat - 25g - (38%)
- Cholesterol - 75mg - (25%)
- Sodium - 2068mg - (86%)
- Fiber - 14g - (56%)

Percent Daily Values are based on a 2000 calorie diet.

Wheat-Free Lasagna

Servings: 6-8

Ingredients

- 4-5 zucchini spiralized using the fuller blades into paper-thin sheets
- 4 cups (600g) minced meat of your choice
- 6 cups (1500g) of pasta sauce
- 2 cups (500g) ricotta cheese
- 4 cups (500g) mozzarella cheese
- 1/2 cup (50g) Parmesan cheese
- 8 eggs
- 1 tbsp basil
- 1 tbsp oregano
- 1 tbsp thyme
- 1 tbsp majoram
- 1 tbsp rosemary powder
- 1 tbsp garlic powder
- 1 tbsp onion powder
- Salt and black pepper to taste

Instructions

1. Place the zucchini sheets on a baking tray and roast for 5-10 minutes until tender. Set aside.
2. In a pan, cook the meat with all the spices. Once cooked, add the pasta sauce and let it simmer to combine the flavors.
3. Mix the ricotta cheese, eggs, parmesan cheese and half of mozzarella cheese in a bowl. Set aside.
4. In an oven-safe tray, add a layer of the tomato-and-meat sauce, topped with zucchini sheets and then the cheese mixture.
5. Repeat the sequence. Bake it at 350 degrees for 30-40 minutes or till all the ingredients (particularly the egg and cheese mixture) are thoroughly cooked.
6. Top it off with the remaining mozzarella cheese and bake for 15 minutes. Serve immediately!

Nutritional Information

- Calories - 959
- Carbohydrates - 44g - (15%)
- Protein - 70g - (140%)
- Total Fat - 56g - (86%)
- Cholesterol - 408mg - (136%)
- Sodium - 2280mg - (95%)
- Fiber - 4g - (16%)

Percent Daily Values are based on a 2000 calorie diet.

Carrots in Mustard Slaw

Servings: 4-6

Ingredients

- 5-6 carrots tightly spiralized
- 5-6 tbsp mustard paste
- 1/4 cup (60ml) extra virgin olive oil
- 1/4 cup (15g) parsley finely chopped
- 1 tbsp chives finely chopped
- 3 tbsp vinegar
- 1-2 tsp orange zest
- Salt as required

Instructions

1. Mix all the ingredients thoroughly in a bowl, except for the spiralized carrots.
2. Add the carrots to the dressing and toss to coat evenly.
3. Let it marinate for 15-30 minutes before serving.

Nutritional Information

- Calories - 235
- Carbohydrates - 12g - (4%)

- Protein - 1g - (2%)
- Total Fat - 20g - (31%)
- Sodium - 285mg - (12%)
- Fiber - 3g - (12%)

Percent Daily Values are based on a 2000 calorie diet.

Roasted Sweet Potato Spirals and Chicken Soup

Servings: 3-4

Ingredients

- 2 sweet potato tightly spiralized.
- 4 cups (500g) minced organic chicken.
- 6 cups (1 1/2 litres) of chicken broth
- 5-6 kale leaves roughly chopped
- 4 green onions sliced
- 2 garlic cloves finely chopped
- 1 tsp ginger finely chopped
- 1 1/2 tsp of chili oil
- 1/2 tsp cumin seeds
- 1 tbsp coconut oil
- 2 1/2 tbsp of soy sauce
- 1 tsp fish sauce optional
- Sea salt and freshly ground black pepper to taste

Instructions

1. In a bowl, marinate chicken with garlic, ginger, chili oil, cumin, salt and black pepper. Mix well and let it sit for a couple of hours.
2. Spiralize the sweet potato, place it on a baking sheet and spray with coconut oil and roast in the oven till crunchy. Place in an air tight container.
3. Heat the coconut oil in a pan and add the meat. Cook thoroughly for 8-10 minutes till slightly browned.
4. Add the broth and let it simmer.

5. Add the kale leaves, green onions, soy sauce and fish sauce and cook for 8-10 minutes. Season to taste with pepper and salt.
6. Dish out into a serving bowl, place the roasted spiralised sweet potato and serve immediately!

Nutritional Information

- Calories - 775
- Carbohydrates - 42g - (14%)
- Protein - 65g - (130%)
- Total Fat - 37g - (57%)
- Cholesterol - 170mg - (57%)
- Sodium - 2442mg - (102%)
- Fiber - 4g - (16%)

Percent Daily Values are based on a 2000 calorie diet.

Zucchini with Avocado Sauce

Servings: 3-4

Ingredients

- 3-4 zucchini tightly spiralized
- 1 tomato diced

For the sauce:

- 1 avocado deseeded and cut into cubes
- 1/4 cup (30g) pumpkin seeds
- 1 cup (40g) fresh basil leaves
- 1 tbsp lemon juice
- 2-3 tbsp olive oil
- Salt and pepper to taste

Instructions

1. Blend the avocado, pumpkin seeds, basil leaves, and lemon juice in a blender.
2. Use the olive oil and 1-2 tbsp of water and mix with the blended ingredients to a smooth the paste. Set the sauce aside.
3. Place the zucchini spirals and tomatoes in a bowl.
4. Add a generous amount of the sauce. Toss and serve.

Nutritional Information

- Calories - 272
- Carbohydrates - 11g - (4%)
- Protein - 6g - (12%)
- Total Fat - 24g - (37%)
- Sodium - 77mg - (3%)
- Fiber - 7g - (28%)

Percent Daily Values are based on a 2000 calorie diet.

Salmon with Spiralized Zucchini

Servings: 3-4

Ingredients

- 8oz (200g) salmon steam-cooked and cut into cubes
- 2-3 zucchini tightly spiralized
- 1 green onion sliced
- 1 onion finely chopped
- 1 cup (240ml) coconut milk
- 1 tbsp lemon juice
- 1/4 tsp cayenne powder optional
- Salt and black pepper to taste

Instructions

1. In a pan, heat some olive oil ensuring the heat is low; cook the onions till fragrant.
2. Add coconut milk, lemon juice, cayenne, pepper and salt and cook for a few minutes.
3. Add the salmon and simmer over a low flame.
4. In another pan, use a vegetable steamer to steam the spiralized zucchini. Do not over-cook.
5. Dish the zucchini spirals on the serving plate.
6. Top it off with a generous amount of salmon sauce.
7. Garnish with green onions and serve.

Nutritional Information

- Calories - 292
- Carbohydrates - 14g - (5%)
- Protein - 19g - (38%)
- Total Fat - 20g - (31%)
- Cholesterol - 35mg - (12%)
- Sodium - 70mg - (3%)
- Fiber - 3g - (12%)

Percent Daily Values are based on a 2000 calorie diet.

Creamy Spiralized Sweet Potato

Servings: 3-4

Ingredients

- 3-4 sweet potatoes tightly spiralized
- 3-4 tbsp butter
- 1 cup (240ml) sour cream
- 1/4 cup (60ml) regular cream
- 1-2 tsp basil dried
- Salt and black pepper to taste

Instructions

1. Heat the butter in a pan. Add the spiralized sweet potatoes and cook for a few minutes.
2. Add the remaining ingredients and stir gently.
3. Remove from heat, dish out into a serving dish and serve.

Nutritional Information

- Calories - 404
- Carbohydrates - 30g - (10%)
- Protein - 5g - (10%)
- Total Fat - 30g - (46%)
- Cholesterol - 72mg - (24%)
- Sodium - 123mg - (5%)
- Fiber - 4g - (16%)

Percent Daily Values are based on a 2000 calorie diet.

Chapter 9 – 10 Spiralized Recipes for Weight Loss

Maintaining a healthy weight is crucial for overall fitness. It does not only help you prevent diseases and medical problems, it also enables you to live a long and fulfilling life. Here are a few recipes to help you lose excess weight to remain fit and healthy.

Spiralized Zucchini with Creamy Cashew Sauce

Servings: 1-2

Ingredients

- 1 medium sized zucchini spiralized

For the Sauce:

- 1 cup (100g) cashew nuts soaked in water for 2 hours
- 2-3 tsp parsley
- 2-3 tsp basil leaves
- 1 tbsp lemon juice
- 1 tsp curry powder
- 1/4 tsp onion powder
- 1/4 tsp garlic powder
- Salt and black pepper to taste

Instructions

For the Sauce:

1. Combine all the ingredients except parsley and basil leaves in the blender.
2. Blend till you get a smooth paste.
3. Add the basil and parsley and pulse briefly to combine.
4. Transfer to an airtight container for storage.

For the Recipe:

1. Spiralize the zucchini, add a little salt and let it stand in the strainer for 30minutes to remove excess water.
2. Rinse off the salt and remove excess water, place into a serving bowl.
3. Add the cashew nut sauce, toss and serve.

Nutritional Information

- Calories - 647
- Carbohydrates - 42g - (14%)

- Protein - 23g - (46%)
- Total Fat - 49g - (75%)
- Sodium - 23mg - (1%)
- Fiber - 7g - (28%)

Percent Daily Values are based on a 2000 calorie diet.

Spicy Vegan Surprise

Servings: 2-3

Ingredients

- 1 zucchini spiralized
- 1 cucumber spiralized
- 1 carrot spiralized
- 1-2 tbsp cilantro (coriander) roughly chopped
- Sunflower seeds for garnish

For Sauce:

- 2 tbsp almond butter
- 2-3 tbsp lemon juice
- 1-2 tsp soy sauce
- 1 garlic clove finely chopped
- 1/2 tsp ginger finely chopped
- 1 pinch of red pepper flakes
- 1 tsp maple syrup

Instructions

For the Sauce:

1. Mix all the ingredients carefully in a bowl. Transfer to an airtight container for storage.

For the Recipe:

1. Place all the ingredients in a bowl, add the sauce and toss.
2. Dish out into a serving bowl and serve.

Nutritional Information

- Calories - 162
- Carbohydrates - 18g - (6%)
- Protein - 5g - (10%)
- Total Fat - 10g - (15%)
- Sodium - 248mg - (10%)
- Fiber - 3g - (12%)

Percent Daily Values are based on a 2000 calorie diet.

Zucchini and Kale Pasta

Servings: 3-4

Ingredients

- 4 zucchini spiralized
- 2 avocados deseeded and cubed
- 1 cup (150g) cherry tomatoes sliced in half
- 4 garlic cloves finely chopped
- 1/4 cup (60ml) olive oil
- 1/4 cup (25g) cheese
- 1/2 cup (70g) pine nuts toasted
- 5-6 kale leaves torn into smaller pieces
- 1 tbsp lemon juice
- Salt and black pepper to taste

Instructions

1. Spiralize the zucchini, rub a little salt, and place in a strainer to drain excess water. Set aside.
2. Blend the garlic, avocado, cheese, pine nuts and lemon juice. Once blended, add the kale leaves and pulse until well mixed.

3. Rinse the zucchini noodles and drained all excess water and dish out onto a serving bowl.
4. Add generous amounts of the blended sauce, toss and serve.

Nutritional Information

- Calories - 613
- Carbohydrates - 33g - (11%)
- Protein - 12g - (24%)
- Total Fat - 53g - (82%)
- Cholesterol - 8mg - (3%)
- Sodium - 148mg - (6%)
- Fiber - 16g - (64%)

Percent Daily Values are based on a 2000 calorie diet.

Spiralized Carrot with Sweet and Sour Ginger Sauce

Servings: 4-6

Ingredients

- 5 carrots tightly spiralized
- 1/2 cup (50g) cashew nuts roasted and crushed
- 2 tbsp cilantro (coriander) roughly chopped

For the Sauce:

- 2 tbsp peanut butter
- 4 tbsp coconut milk
- 2 tbsp soy sauce
- 1/4 tsp cayenne pepper
- 2-3 garlic cloves finely chopped
- 1 tbsp ginger finely chopped
- 1 tbsp lemon juice
- Salt and black pepper to taste

Instructions

For the Sauce:

1. Combine all the ingredients in a bowl and mix thoroughly.
2. Transfer to an airtight container for later.

For the Pasta:

1. Place the remaining ingredients in a bowl.
2. Add the sauce and toss well.
3. Dish out into a serving bowl and garnish with the chopped cilantro and crushed cashew nuts.
4. Serve immediately.

Nutritional Information

- Calories - 194
- Carbohydrates - 16g - (5%)
- Protein - 6g - (12%)
- Total Fat - 13g - (20%)
- Sodium - 553mg - (23%)
- Fiber - 4g - (16%)

Percent Daily Values are based on a 2000 calorie diet.

Spiralized Egg Plant

Servings: 1-2

Ingredients

- 1 eggplant spiralized
- 1 garlic clove finely chopped
- 1 cup (150g) cherry tomatoes sliced in quarters
- 1/4 cup (60g) chickpeas
- 1 tbsp raisins

- 1/4 tsp red pepper flakes
- 1/4 tsp oregano
- 1 tbsp olive oil
- Salt and black pepper to taste

Instructions

1. In a pan, add olive oil and heat gently.
2. Add garlic and sauté till fragrant.
3. Add the red pepper flakes and cook for half a minute.
4. Add the chickpeas, tomatoes and raisins and cook for 5-7.
5. Add the spiralized eggplant, salt, pepper and oregano. Stir carefully.
6. Dish out and serve!

Nutritional Information

- Calories - 528
- Carbohydrates - 87g - (29%)
- Protein - 15g - (30%)
- Total Fat - 20g - (31%)
- Sodium - 121mg - (5%)
- Fiber - 43g - (172%)

Percent Daily Values are based on a 2000 calorie diet.

Zucchini with Avocado and Walnut Sauce

Servings: 2-3

Ingredients

- 3 zucchini spiralized
- 1 tomato diced
- 1/2 avocado cubed
- 2 tbsp parsley
- 1 garlic clove finely chopped
- 2 tsp lemon juice

- 1 tsp extra virgin olive oil
- 1 tsp basil
- 1 tbsp walnuts crushed

Instructions

1. In a blender, mix the avocado, parsley, garlic, lemon juice, olive oil, basil, and walnuts.
2. Pulse repeatedly to get a crunchy paste. Add a little water, if required.
3. Heat the sauce slightly in a pan.
4. Place the spiralized zucchini and add tomatoes in a bowl, add in the heated sauce and toss to coat evenly.
5. Serve immediately.

Nutritional Information

- Calories - 170
- Carbohydrates - 18g - (6%)
- Protein - 6g - (12%)
- Total Fat - 11g - (17%)
- Sodium - 39mg - (2%)
- Fiber - 8g - (32%)

Percent Daily Values are based on a 2000 calorie diet.

Tangy Carrot Pasta

Servings: 1-2

Ingredients

- 1 large carrot tightly spiralized

For the Sauce:

- 1 tbsp tahini paste
- 1 tbsp olive oil

- 3 tbsp lemon juice
- 1 tsp soy sauce
- 1 tsp ginger finely chopped
- 1 garlic clove finely chopped

Instructions

For the Sauce:

1. Combine all the ingredients carefully in a bowl.
2. Transfer to an airtight container for use later.

For the Pasta:

1. Tightly spiralize carrots and transfer into a serving bowl.
2. Add the sauce and toss well.
3. Serve immediately.

Nutritional Information

- Calories - 214
- Carbohydrates - 13g - (4%)
- Protein - 2g - (4%)
- Total Fat - 18g - (28%)
- Sodium - 417mg - (17%)
- Fiber - 3g - (12%)

Percent Daily Values are based on a 2000 calorie diet.

Meaty Zucchini Surprise

Servings: 2-3

Ingredients

- 3 zucchini spiralized
- 1/2 cup (70g) meat sliced in strips

- 1 garlic clove finely chopped
- 1/4 tsp red pepper flakes
- 1/2 cup (50g) mixed cheese
- Salt and black pepper to taste

Instructions

1. Heat some oil in a pan and cook the meat thoroughly.
2. When cooked, transfer to a plate.
3. In the same pan, add some more oil and cook garlic and red chili flakes for 30 seconds.
4. Add the spiralized zucchini and cook for 2-3 minutes.
5. Add the remaining ingredients, toss carefully.
6. Dish out into a serving bowl, sprinkle the cheese over the top.
7. Serve immediately!

Nutritional Information

- Calories - 244
- Carbohydrates - 12g - (4%)
- Protein - 19g - (38%)
- Total Fat - 15g - (23%)
- Cholesterol - 53mg - (18%)
- Sodium - 429mg - (18%)
- Fiber - 3g - (12%)

Percent Daily Values are based on a 2000 calorie diet.

Thai-Inspired Zucchini Pasta

Servings: 1-2

Ingredients

- 2 zucchini tightly spiralized
- 1 garlic clove finely chopped
- 1 green onion sliced

- 2 eggs scrambled
- 1 tbsp corn flour
- 1/4 cup (35g) peanuts roasted
- 1/2 tbsp almond oil
- 1 tbsp cilantro roughly chopped

For the Sauce:

- 2 tbsp lemon juice
- 1 tbsp fish sauce
- 1/2 tbsp soy sauce
- 1 tbsp chili sauce
- 1 tsp honey

Instructions

For the Sauce:

1. Combine all the ingredients and mixed thoroughly in a bowl.
2. Transfer to an airtight container to be used later.

For the Recipe:

1. In a pan, add some oil, add the garlic and green onions.
2. Sauté briefly till the green onion softens.
3. Add the sauce prepared earlier and mix thoroughly.
4. Add the corn flour while stirring. The sauce will begin to thicken.
5. Cook for 2-3 minute until the desired consistency is obtained.
6. Add the spiralized zucchini and chopped cilantro to this mixture.
7. Stir to coat evenly and cook for about 1 minute to combine the flavors.
8. Remove from heat, dish out on to a serving dish, place the scrambled eggs and nuts on the top.
9. Serve immediately.

Nutritional Information

- Calories - 586
- Carbohydrates - 49g - (16%)

- Protein - 28g - (56%)
- Total Fat - 35g - (54%)
- Cholesterol - 372mg - (124%)
- Sodium - 2493mg - (104%)
- Fiber - 9g - (36%)

Percent Daily Values are based on a 2000 calorie diet.

Zucchini Pasta with Eggs

Servings: 2-3

Ingredients

- 3 zucchini tightly spiralized
- 2 eggs
- 1/2 cup (70g) sliced organic pork
- 1/4 cup (25g) onion chopped
- 1/4 tsp red chili flakes
- 1 garlic clove finely chopped
- 1 tbsp olive oil
- 1/2 cup (50g) Parmesan cheese
- Salt and pepper to taste

Instructions

1. In a pan, heat the olive oil gently.
2. Add garlic and red chili flakes and sauté for 1 minute.
3. Add the onions and cook for 2-3 minutes or until soft.
4. Add the sliced pork and cook thoroughly.
5. Add the spiralized zucchini, salt and pepper and mix thoroughly.
6. Cook the eggs in a separate pan, scramble eggs.
7. Dish out the zucchini and meat mixture into your serving bowl.
8. Top it off with parmesan cheese and the scrambled egg.
9. Serve immediately.

Nutritional Information

- Calories - 381
- Carbohydrates - 14g - (5%)
- Protein - 28g - (56%)
- Total Fat - 25g - (38%)
- Cholesterol - 238mg - (79%)
- Sodium - 608mg - (25%)
- Fiber - 4g - (16%)

Percent Daily Values are based on a 2000 calorie diet.

Chapter 10 – Nutritional Insight about the Spiralized Fruits and Vegetables used in the Recipes

I've used quite a few spiralized ingredients in this book to create some wonderful recipes. The most popular vegetables, by far, are zucchini, sweet potato, carrots, and bell peppers. Here are some of the nutritional insights about these vegetables that will help you make a positive change to your meals.

Zucchini

Zucchini is widely preferred for spiralizing because it does not need to be cooked before consumption. It is perfectly fine to consume zucchini in its raw form, as shown in some of my recipes.

The high fibre content in Zucchini helps in maintaining a healthy gut. Besides this, zucchini possesses anti-oxidant properties that help in weight loss and disease prevention. It is also known to have anti-aging properties. It is a good source of minerals and vitamins, which is why it is recommended for daily use.

There are several varieties of zucchini, and they all have similar health benefits:

- Protect against infections and diseases and maintains good health.
- Help to maintain a healthy heart.
- Help to prevent cancer.
- A useful tool for weight reduction.
- Help with reducing inflammation and beneficial for reducing arthritic aches.

Sweet Potato

Sweet potatoes are generally preferred for their special taste. It is easy to spiralize and can be consumed in its raw form as well.

Sweet potato is known to be one of the most energy-packed root vegetables. It contains a wide assortment of nutrients with several health benefits.

- It is rich in beta-carotene which may reduce the risk of developing certain types of cancer, and delay aging and body degeneration.
- Supports eye health.
- Low glycaemic index food which helps to stabilize blood glucose levels especially in patients with diabetes.
- Helps to maintain normal healthy blood pressure because of the potassium content.
- Improves heart health.
- The high fibre content may help with prevention of constipation.
- Boosts the immune system.

Carrots

Carrots are one of the healthiest vegetables that are consumed in their raw form. It is easy to spiralize and can be consumed in any form.

There are several health benefits of consuming carrots. These include:

- Boosting the immune system
- Facilitating digestion
- Maintaining healthy blood pressure
- Regulating blood sugar levels
- Improving eye sight
- Preventing cancers
- Lowering the risk of heart diseases and macular degeneration
- Reducing the risk of strokes and other medical problems
- Promoting healthy gums and teeth
- And lots more!

Carrots consumed in any form – raw, steamed, juiced, or any other form – provide an essential mix of nutrients that can serve as a pick-me-up. Consuming carrots on a daily basis can keep several problems at bay!

Bell Peppers

The crunchy texture of capsicum or bell pepper, make them an exciting addition to salads. There's a wide variety of bell peppers available for use. Each variety seems to have a different set of characteristics which makes them interesting for most food enthusiasts.

Besides this, bell peppers are known to have the following health benefits:

- A rich source of carotenoids, the nutrients that are known to promote heart health.
- They contain high amounts of antioxidants, promoting longevity and anti-aging.
- Bell peppers are known to have anti-inflammatory properties.
- The nutritional combination of bell peppers promote heart health and control diabetes.
- This vegetable fights cancerous cells and other diseases, ensuring overall health and fitness.
- Bell peppers contain an assortment of vitamins and minerals that help in improving vision and protecting the eyes against age-related problems.

Apples

The recommendation is to consume an apple everyday in order to maintain optimal health and fitness; as they say, "An apple a day keeps the doctor away!"

It is one of the most common fruits widely preferred for their texture and flavor. Apples contain a wide assortment of nutrients that offer an amazing start to the day.

The health benefits of apples include:

- Healthier and whiter teeth
- Boosting memory and brain function
- Lowering the risk of cancers
- Managing blood sugar levels
- Reducing cholesterol levels and promoting heart health
- Maintaining healthy gut
- Promoting weight loss
- Boosting the immune system
- Improving eye sight and preventing long term problems.
- Apples are known to have anti-aging properties and help in keeping the skin smooth and healthy.

Jicama

Jicama is a root vegetable which is low in calories; it contains a soluble fibre called oligofructose a sub group of inulin. It gives the root a sweet flavour. It is not metabolized in the body and therefore does not increase the glucose level in the blood and it does not stimulate the secretion of insulin. This is what makes it an ideal sweet snack for diabetics and those wanting to lose weight. It contains various vitamins and minerals that help maintaining good health.

The health benefits of Jicama are:

- boosts the immune system, could reduce the risks of cancer.
- supports eye and skin health,
- helps with anti-inflammatory conditions.
- Help with weight loss
- Manage blood glucose levels and help with diabetes.
- The soluble fibre can aid the reduction of cholesterol levels and help maintain heart health

Final Note

Add more spiralized fruits and vegetables to your daily intake. Use different spiralizer blades to add a twist to your recipes everyday! Continue experimenting as that will make food preparation more interesting. There's a whole world of vegetables and fruits waiting to be spiralized.

Have fun with your spiralizer and enjoy more vegetables.

15751389R00053

Printed in Great Britain
by Amazon